W9-CXU-562

BIGGEST NAMES IN SPORTS
BUBBA WALLACE
AUTO RACING STAR

by Connor Stratton

FOCUS
READERS.

NAVIGATOR

WWW.FOCUSREADERS.COM

Focus Readers is distributed by North Star Editions:
sales@northstareditions.com | 888-417-0195

Produced for Focus Readers by Red Line Editorial.

Photographs ©: Paul Sancya/AP Images, cover, 1; Alex Menendez/AP Images, 4–5; Phelan M. Ebenhack/AP Images, 7; Jerry Markland/Getty Images Sport/Getty Images, 8–9; Shutterstock Images, 11; Nigel Kinrade/Autostock/AP Images, 13; Nigel Kinrade/NKP/AP Images, 14–15, 19, 27; Matt Slocum/AP Images, 17; Russell LaBounty/NKP/AP Images, 20–21; Evan Frost/Minnesota Public Radio/AP Images, 23; Steve Helber/AP Images, 25; Red Line Editorial, 29

Library of Congress Cataloging-in-Publication Data
Names: Stratton, Connor, author.
Title: Bubba Wallace : auto racing star / by Connor Stratton.
Description: Lake Elmo, MN : Focus Readers, 2021. | Series: Biggest names in
  sports | Includes index. | Audience: Grades 4-6
Identifiers: LCCN 2020039723 (print) | LCCN 2020039724 (ebook) | ISBN
  9781644937037 (Hardcover) | ISBN 9781644937396 (Paperback) | ISBN
  9781644938119 (PDF) | ISBN 9781644937754 (eBook)
Subjects: LCSH: Wallace, Bubba, 1993---Juvenile literature. | Automobile
  racing drivers--United States--Biography--Juvenile literature. | African
  American athletes--United States--Biography--Juvenile literature. |
  African American athletes--Political activity--History--21st century. |
  Racism in sports--Juvenile literature. | NASCAR (Association)--History.
Classification: LCC GV1032.W34 S87 2021 (print) | LCC GV1032.W34 (ebook)
  | DDC 796.720973 [B]--dc23
LC record available at https://lccn.loc.gov/2020039723
LC ebook record available at https://lccn.loc.gov/2020039724

Printed in the United States of America
Mankato, MN
012021

ABOUT THE AUTHOR

Connor Stratton writes and edits children's books. Raised just outside the Windy City, he loves all things Bears, Cubs, Blackhawks, and Bulls. He was unlucky enough to attend the ill-fated Bartman game in 2003, and he was glad when the 2016 team laid the Cubs' curse to rest. He lives in Minnesota.

TABLE OF CONTENTS

CHAPTER 1

MAKING HISTORY AT DAYTONA

Bubba Wallace sped along the inside lane of the Daytona International Speedway. Wallace was taking part in NASCAR's biggest event of the year. Only two laps remained at the 2018 Daytona 500. Wallace's No. 43 car trailed behind the leaders. But it was still anyone's race.

Bubba Wallace greets fans before racing in the 2018 Daytona 500.

Suddenly, two cars in the pack made contact with each other. One car spun out and crashed into several cars behind it. Wallace quickly dropped down along the **apron**. Sparks flew from his car. But he avoided the wreck and stayed in the race.

Usually, the Daytona 500 lasts for 200 laps. However, NASCAR doesn't allow a race to end under **caution**. As a result, officials added two extra laps.

Going into the final lap, Wallace was in fourth place. He tailed Austin Dillon, who was in second. Then Dillon bumped into the back of Aric Almirola, the leader. Almirola smashed into the wall, and Dillon shot ahead to take the lead.

Wallace (43) steers clear of a dangerous wreck during the 2018 Daytona 500.

Wallace followed close behind. He edged out another car for a second-place finish.

Wallace had been hoping to win his first Daytona 500. But even with a second-place finish, he proved that he was one of NASCAR's best young drivers. He also made history. Wallace was the first Black driver at the Daytona 500 in nearly 50 years.

CHAPTER 2

GO-KARTS TO RACE TRUCKS

Darrell "Bubba" Wallace Jr. was born in Mobile, Alabama, on October 8, 1993. His mother was Black, and his father was white. When he was a baby, his sister started calling him Bubba. The nickname stuck. When Bubba was two years old, the family moved to Concord, North Carolina. NASCAR was very popular there.

A 16-year-old Bubba Wallace attends a NASCAR event aimed at increasing diversity in the sport.

Bubba loved racing from an early age. He started racing go-karts at nine years old. He quickly changed to Bandoleros. These cars are similar to the stock cars that NASCAR drivers use. But Bandoleros are tiny.

Bubba didn't notice much **racism** in the sport at first. That changed when he was 13 years old. Another driver's parent called him a racist name. Bubba's mother explained that these experiences would continue if he stayed in racing. After all, NASCAR was one of the least diverse sports in the United States.

However, Bubba loved driving too much to stop. He continued to race, and his

Bandoleros can reach speeds of more than 60 miles per hour (97 km/h).

effort paid off. In 2010, Bubba started competing in a regional NASCAR **series**. As a 16-year-old, he became the youngest driver to win in that series.

In 2012, Wallace competed for the first time in the NASCAR Xfinity Series.

That is the sport's second-highest series. And in 2013, he started competing in NASCAR's truck-racing series. He won his first truck race that October. He became the first Black driver to win a national-series race in nearly 50 years.

DRIVING WHILE BLACK

Bubba survived racism off the racetrack, too. Police officers pulled him over many times. Officers often suggested that Bubba had stolen his own car. Bubba worried that the police might shoot him. These experiences were not unique to him. US police officers are much more likely to pull over Black drivers than white drivers. In addition, Black people are more likely to be shot by police during traffic stops.

Wallace takes a practice lap before a NASCAR Truck Series race in 2013.

Wallace's truck-racing success earned him a full-time ride in the Xfinity Series. In 2015 and 2016, he notched top-10 finishes in more than 20 races. His shot at NASCAR's top Cup Series was just around the corner.

CHAPTER 3

DRIVING NO. 43

Going into 2017, Bubba Wallace wasn't sure if he would be able to race a full season. His Xfinity Series **sponsor** had funded him for only part of the year. But in May 2017, a Cup Series driver became injured. Wallace knew this could be his chance. He reached out to the driver's team, Richard Petty Motorsports (RPM).

Wallace (6) leads the pack during a 2017 Xfinity Series race in Las Vegas, Nevada.

He told the team he could fill in, and he got the job.

Wallace had earned a place in the sport's top series. He would be racing for RPM's owner, Richard Petty himself. Petty was known as "the King." He had won the most NASCAR races in history. Wallace even got to use Petty's famous No. 43.

Wallace's first test was at Pocono Raceway in Pennsylvania. However, the race didn't go well. On more than one occasion, Wallace drove too fast while making a **pit stop**. These mistakes led to penalties, and he finished 26th.

However, Wallace raced No. 43 a few more times that season. And each race,

Wallace shares a laugh with racing legend Richard Petty.

he finished in a better position. Petty was impressed. So, he hired Wallace to race full-time in 2018. Wallace had made history once again. He became the second Black driver to race full-time in NASCAR's top series.

In 2018, Wallace performed well on and off the track. He came off as likable with reporters. Wallace's talent with the media attracted new sponsors. In auto racing, sponsors provide more than just income. Their money also goes toward improving

NASCAR'S FIRST BLACK DRIVER

Wendell Scott was the first Black driver to compete full-time at NASCAR's top level. He raced in the Cup Series for most of the 1960s. Scott experienced a great deal of racism in the sport. In fact, several racetracks did not let him compete because he was Black. Even so, Scott finished many seasons in the top 10. And in 1963, he became the first Black driver to win a national-series race.

Wallace makes a pit stop during a 2018 race at Michigan International Speedway.

the driver's car. That way, the car runs as fast as possible.

Unfortunately for the RPM team, Wallace didn't put up a first-place finish in 2018. He struggled to win again in 2019. Going into 2020, Wallace knew he had to step up as a leader in the sport.

CHAPTER 4

NASCAR ACTIVIST

Bubba Wallace's 2020 season started out strong. In his first four races, he finished in the top 20 three times. At a race in Las Vegas, he finished sixth. But in March, the COVID-19 virus hit the United States. In response, NASCAR decided not to hold any races for several weeks.

Wallace (43) races in the 2020 Daytona 500.

NASCAR started up again in May. However, racing began to take a back seat for Wallace. That month, a video appeared online. It showed two white men attacking Ahmaud Arbery, an unarmed Black man. Arbery died from a gunshot wound. Two weeks later, an unarmed

FAMILY HORROR

In 2003, a police officer fatally shot Wallace's 19-year-old cousin. Wallace's cousin, who was Black, had been unarmed. He was reaching for his cell phone, and the officer thought he was reaching for a gun. Wallace was only nine years old at the time. In 2020, after the deaths of Ahmaud Arbery and George Floyd, Wallace thought about his cousin. He believed his cousin's death had been similar.

Protesters in Minneapolis, Minnesota, gather at the spot where George Floyd died.

Black man named George Floyd died after being pinned to the ground by a white police officer. The officer was charged with murder. Huge protests against **police brutality** spread across the United States.

These events had a big impact on Wallace. He felt he should start speaking out against racism. He supported the protests online. He asked other NASCAR drivers to speak up, too. And in June, Wallace took a bigger step. He called for a ban on Confederate flags at races.

During the US Civil War (1861–1865), the Confederate states used this flag. The leaders of these states wanted to keep slavery legal. The Confederate states lost the war, and slavery ended in the United States. But many white people kept using Confederate flags. The flag's connection with slavery made the flag especially painful for Black people.

For decades, NASCAR fans had flown Confederate flags at races. Wallace

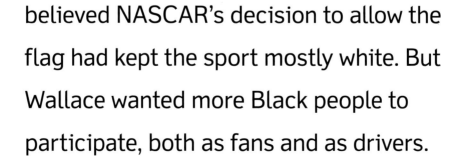

Wallace poses next to his car before a race in June 2020.

believed NASCAR's decision to allow the flag had kept the sport mostly white. But Wallace wanted more Black people to participate, both as fans and as drivers.

Two days after Wallace called for the ban, NASCAR agreed to stop allowing the flag. And at the next race, Wallace's car featured a Black Lives Matter logo.

Wallace received plenty of positive attention for his **activism**. But two weeks later, in Wallace's racing garage, a member of his team found a rope that looked like a noose. Nooses are a symbol of racist violence. Wallace worried that the noose was meant for him. He thought someone was suggesting that he should stop speaking out.

The US government looked into the issue. It found that the noose had been in the garage for several months. It had not

After the noose incident, fellow drivers pushed Wallace's car to the starting line to show their support for him.

been meant for Wallace. Wallace felt safer knowing that he wasn't the target.

Still, Wallace knew his activism had upset certain fans. But he believed his actions had welcomed new fans to the sport. For Wallace, that made the struggle worth it.

BUBBA WALLACE

- Birth date: October 8, 1993
- Birthplace: Mobile, Alabama
- High school: Northwest Cabarrus High School (Concord, North Carolina)
- NASCAR Series: K&N Pro Series East (2010–2012); Gander RV & Outdoors Truck Series (2013–2014, 2017); Xfinity Series (2012, 2014–2017); Cup Series (2017–)
- NASCAR Cup Series Car: Richard Petty Motorsports, No. 43 (2017–2020); new team owned by Michael Jordan (2021–)
- Major awards: K&N Pro Series East Rookie of the Year (2010); Byrnsie Award (2020)

Concord

Daytona Beach

Mobile

FOCUS ON
BUBBA WALLACE

Write your answers on a separate piece of paper.

1. Write a paragraph explaining the main ideas of Chapter 4.

2. What important issues would you want to speak out about? Why?

3. When did Wallace compete in his first Cup Series race?

    A. 2017
    B. 2018
    C. 2020

4. Why do NASCAR drivers need sponsors to win races?

    A. Drivers are not allowed to compete without sponsors.
    B. Drivers with sponsors start a few laps ahead of other drivers.
    C. Sponsors help pay for the costs of building fast race cars.

Answer key on page 32.

GLOSSARY

activism
Actions to make social or political changes.

apron
The part of a racetrack that divides the racing lanes from the inside of the track.

caution
Laps of an auto race when it's not safe to drive, often happening after a crash.

pit stop
A stop a driver makes during an auto race to make repairs or get more fuel.

police brutality
When a police officer uses more force than necessary against civilians.

racism
Hatred or mistreatment of people because of their skin color or ethnicity.

series
A set of races among various teams that compete during a season.

sponsor
A company that pays a team to advertise its products.

TO LEARN MORE

BOOKS

Goldsworthy, Steve. *The Tech Behind Race Cars*. North Mankato, MN: Capstone Press, 2020.

Harris, Duchess, and Cynthia Kennedy Henzel. *Politics and Protest in Sports*. Minneapolis: Abdo Publishing, 2019.

Rule, Heather. *Ultimate NASCAR Road Trip*. Minneapolis: Abdo Publishing, 2019.

NOTE TO EDUCATORS

Visit **www.focusreaders.com** to find lesson plans, activities, links, and other resources related to this title.

INDEX

Answer Key: **1.** Answers will vary; **2.** Answers will vary; **3.** A; **4.** C